**Safety First!**

# Safety on the School Bus

by Lucia Raatma

**Consultant:**
Karen E. Finkel, Executive Director
National School Transportation Association

Bridgestone Books
an imprint of Capstone Press
Mankato, Minnesota

Bridgestone Books are published by Capstone Press
818 North Willow Street, Mankato, Minnesota 56001
http://www.capstone-press.com

*Library of Congress Cataloging-in-Publication Data*
Raatma, Lucia.
Safety on the school bus/by Lucia Raatma.
    p.  cm.—(Safety first)
Includes bibliographical references (p. 24) and index.
Summary: Explains how to be safe while waiting for, getting on and off, and riding the
school bus.
ISBN 0-7368-0063-8
1. School children—Transportation—Safety measures—Juvenile literature.
2. School buses—Safety measures—Juvenile literature. [1. School buses. 2. Safety.]
I. Title. II. Series.
LB2864.R22  1999
363.12′59—dc21
                                                                        98-19592
                                                                            CIP
                                                                            AC

**Editorial Credits**
Rebecca Glaser, editor; Clay Schotzko/Icon Productions, cover designer;
   Sheri Gosewisch, photo researcher

**Photo Credits**
Barbara Stitzer, 4, 6, 8, 10, 12, 14, 16, 18, 20
Unicorn Stock Photos/Tom McCarthy, cover

# Table of Contents

PUBLIC SCHOOLS

## The School Bus

The school bus is a safe way to get to school. The school bus picks up children near their homes. It takes children home after school. You can learn how to be safe on the school bus.

## The Bus Stop

You can be safe while you wait at your bus stop. Arrive at your bus stop early. Wait at the bus stop with others if you can. This is safer than waiting alone.

## Staying Back from the Bus

School bus drivers cannot see children who are close to buses. Stay back from the bus so the bus driver can see you. You may need to cross the street. Walk in front of a stopped bus if you do. The driver cannot see you behind the bus.

## Getting on the School Bus

The driver will open the doors after the bus stops. Wait your turn to get on the bus. Hold the hand rail as you step onto the bus. Find a seat quickly so others behind you may sit down.

## The School Bus Driver

The school bus driver keeps children safe. Always listen to the bus driver. Talk quietly so you do not bother the driver. The driver must pay attention while driving the school bus.

## On the School Bus

The driver may need to stop the bus quickly. Stay in your seat while on the bus. You could fall forward if you are standing or kneeling. Keep your arms and head inside the bus. Do not put things in the aisle between the seats.

EMERGENCY DOOR
SEE   INSTRUCTIONS   BELOW

## Emergencies

An emergency is a sudden danger like a crash or fire. Stay still and listen to the driver during an emergency. The driver may tell you to go to an emergency exit. You should know where the emergency exits are.

## Getting off the School Bus

Do not stand up until the bus has stopped.
Do not push to get off the bus. Make sure
your clothes and book bag do not have long
strings. These strings can become caught
in the door. Hold the hand rail as you leave
the bus. You could slip and fall if you do not.

## After You Leave the School Bus

You should follow safety rules after you get off the school bus. Stay back from the bus. Do not push others near the bus. Someone could get hurt. Walk into school with other people to stay safe.

# Hands on: Play the Alphabet Game

The school bus driver needs to pay attention. Loud noises bother the driver. But you can play quiet games like this one.

## What You Do

1. Sit near other children who want to play. Players should sit on each side of the bus.
2. Look out the windows. See if you can find something that starts with A. One example is an airplane. Tell the others what you saw. Only things that are outside your bus count.
3. Then, try to find something that starts with B. One example is a bicycle.
4. Look for things that start with each letter of the alphabet. Each person should find a different thing for each letter.
5. Play until you get to the end of the alphabet. Or play until you leave the bus.
6. Whoever gets farthest or reaches the end of the alphabet first wins.

# Words to Know

**aisle** (ILE)—a walkway between seats

**bus stop** (BUHSS STOP)—a place where people wait for a bus

**emergency** (i-MUHR-juhn-see)—a sudden danger like a crash or fire

**kneel** (NEEL)—to sit on one's knees

# Read More

**Loewen, Nancy.** *School Safety.* Plymouth, Minn.: Child's World, 1997.

**Ready, Dee.** *School Bus Drivers.* Community Helpers. Mankato, Minn.: Bridgestone Books, 1998.

**Ready, Dee.** *School Buses.* Early-Reader Science: Transportation. Mankato, Minn.: Bridgestone Books, 1998.

# Internet Sites

**National School Transportation Association**

http://www.schooltrans.com

**NHTSA's Safety City Bus Safety**

http://www.nhtsa.dot.gov/kids/bussafety/index.html

**School Bus Safety**

http://www.cammarata.com/schoolbus.html

# Index